A Rookie reader®

Being Me

Written by Julie Broski
Illustrated by Vincent Vigla

Children's Press®
A Division of Scholastic Inc.
New York • Toronto • London • Auckland • Sydney
Mexico City • New Delhi • Hong Kong
Danbury, Connecticut

For the children, families, and staff of the Children's Center for the Visually Impaired
in Kansas City and Infant Toddler Services of Johnson County. You are all amazing!
—J.B.

For Marie and Maria
—V.V.

Reading Consultant

Eileen Robinson
Reading Specialist

Library of Congress Cataloging-in-Publication Data

Broski, Julie, 1962-
  Being me / written by Julie Broski ; illustrated by Vincent Vigla.
    p. cm. — (A rookie reader)
  Summary: A young girl tells what it is like being her, describing the things she likes to do.
  ISBN 0-516-24975-4 (lib. bdg.)   0-516-24913-4 (pbk.)
  [1. Self-perception—Fiction. 2. Self-esteem—Fiction.] I. Vigla, Vincent, 1970- ill. II. Title. III. Series.
  PZ7.B7995175Bei 2006
  [E]—dc22
                          2005016151

CHILDREN'S PRESS, and A ROOKIE READER®, and associated logos are trademarks and/or
registered trademarks of Scholastic Library Publishing. SCHOLASTIC and associated logos
are trademarks and/or registered trademarks of Scholastic Inc.
1 2 3 4 5 6 7 8 9 10 R 15 14 13 12 11 10 09 08 07 06

I like playing dress up.
It's fun being me.

I can add and subtract.
I'm learning lots being me!

I like painting.
That's part of being me.

I can do cartwheels.
Watch out, I'm being me!

I like playing with friends.
I'm happy being me.

11

I help with chores.
I'm busy being me!

13

I like watching clouds.
It's peaceful being me.

I love reading.
It's exciting being me.

17

I enjoy planting flowers.
That's part of being me.

19

I love chocolate chip cookies.
I get hungry being me!

21

I can't hear.
That's part of being me.

23

I talk with my hands.
It's amazing being me.

We are so much alike,
but we have differences, too.

I love you for being you.

I know you love me for just being me.

31

Word List (63 Words)

(Words in **bold** are story words that are repeated throughout the text.)

add	flowers	much
alike	for	my
amazing	friends	of
and	fun	out
are	get	painting
being	hands	part
busy	happy	peaceful
but	have	planting
can	hear	playing
can't	help	reading
cartwheels	hungry	so
chip	I	subtract
chocolate	**I'm**	talk
chores	**it's**	that's
clouds	just	too
cookies	know	up
differences	learning	watch
do	**like**	watching
dress	lots	we
enjoy	**love**	with
exciting	**me**	you

About the Author

Julie Broski is a meteorologist for KCTV5 in Kansas City and an educator. She lives in Kansas City, Kansas, with her husband, John, and three daughters.

About the Illustrator

Vincent Vigla was born in a very pretty, small, old town near Normandy, France. He was a happy child and often dreamt of trains and boats. Since he was very bad in math, Vincent studied graphics at the E.S.A.G.-Penninghen School in Paris. While there, he dreamed of one day working with American and British publishers.